WISCONSIN

in words and pictures

BY DENNIS B. FRADIN

ILLUSTRATIONS BY ROBERT ULM

Consultant
Howard W. Kanetzke
Editor, *Badger History*
State Historical Society of Wisconsin

 **CHILDRENS PRESS, CHICAGO**

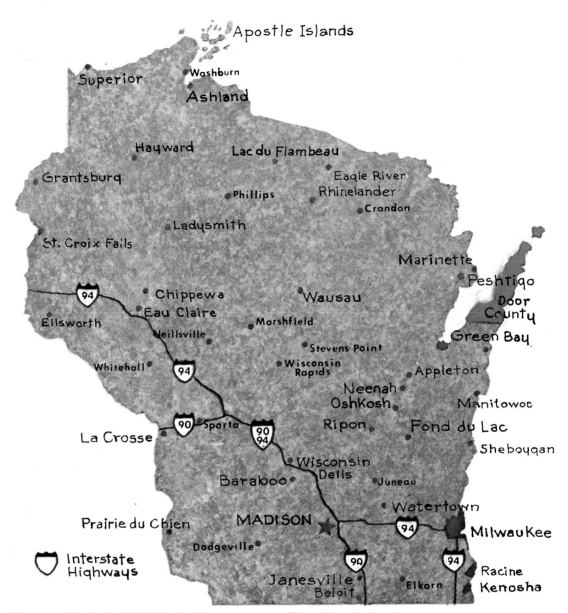

Apostle Islands

Superior
Washburn
Ashland

Hayward
Lac du Flambeau

Grantsburg
Eagle River
Rhinelander
Phillips
Crandon

Ladysmith

St. Croix Fails

Marinette

Chippewa
Wausau
Peshtigo
Door
County
Eau Claire
Marshfield
Ellsworth
Neillsville
Green Bay
Stevens Point
Whitehall
Wisconsin
Rapids
Appleton

Neenah
OshKosh
Manitowoc

Ripon
Fond du Lac

La Crosse
Sparta
Sheboygan

Wisconsin
Dells
Baraboo
Juneau

Prairie du Chien
Watertown

MADISON
Milwaukee
Dodgeville

Interstate
Highways
Janesville
Elkorn
Racine
Beloit
Kenosha

Library of Congress Cataloging in Publication Data

Fradin, Dennis.
    Wisconsin in words and pictures.

    SUMMARY: A brief introduction to the land,
history, cities, industries, folklore, and famous
sites of the Badger State.
    1. Wisconsin—Juvenile literature. [1. Wiscon-
sin] I. Ulm, Robert. II. Title.
F581.3.F73   977.5   77-5330
ISBN 0-516-03948-2

Picture Acknowledgments:
WISCONSIN DEPARTMENT OF NATURAL RESOURCES—cover, 7, 10,
    15, 30, 31, 41, 43
UNIVERSITY OF WISCONSIN-EXTENSION PROGRAM - 19, 32, 38(left)
    44
WISCONSIN DIVISION OF TOURISM—24, 27, 29, 38
WISCONSIN DAIRIES CO-OP, James R. Hasse—25
MILWAUKEE BOARD OF HARBOR COMMISSIONERS—28
MARINETTE AREA CHAMBER OF COMMERCE, Joe Paradis—36

COVER PICTURE: Eagle Bluff, Peninsula State Park on Lake Michigan

Wisconsin (wis • KAHN • sin) comes from the Chippewa (CHIP • ih • wah) Indian word "Wees-Konsan"—meaning "the gathering of waters." Wisconsin is a state of sparkling rivers and lakes. It also has vast forests, rich farmland, and the big city of Milwaukee (mill • WAW • kee).

Do you know what state gives us the most milk? Where the first kindergarten in America began? Where the first auto race was held? As you will see, the answer to all these questions is—Wisconsin!

Millions of years ago there was no state of Wisconsin. There were no people here. Huge animals called *mammoths* (MAM•uths) ruled the land.

About a million years ago the weather turned cold. Mountains of ice called *glaciers* (GLAY•shers) moved down from the north and covered most of Wisconsin. The glaciers crushed almost everything in their path. They turned Wisconsin into flat land—good for forests and farms.

The ice came and went four times. Finally the Ice Age ended. The glaciers melted, leaving behind a gift for Wisconsin: thousands of lovely lakes.

Very little is known about the first people here. One early group is known as the Effigy (EFF•ih•gee) Mound Builders.

The Mound Builders lived here over 1200 years ago. They left no written record. But from their tools we can tell that they knew how to farm. They also built thousands of dirt mounds throughout a big area that includes Wisconsin. Bones and pottery have been found inside the smaller mounds. These were used as burial places.

A few of the mounds are very big. They are shaped like buffaloes, snakes, wolves, deer, and even a giant man. Why were the mounds built? That is still a mystery.

Scientists think that the Mound Builders were related to the Indians who came later.

Indians gathering wild rice

Many tribes of Indians lived in Wisconsin. The Chippewa (CHIP•ih•wah) tribe lived in the cold north woods. They ate wild rice and hunted for deer. They wore clothes made of deer skin. The Chippewa Indians were also great fishermen.

The Menominee (men•OM•in•ee) tribe lived near the rivers and lakes. They made canoes from the bark of birch trees. They used birch bark to build their wigwams, too. When the Frenchmen came, they called them "wild rice eaters."

The Potawatomi (pot•ah•WHAT•om•ee) and
Winnebago (win•eh•BAY•go) tribes lived in the southern
half of Wisconsin. They grew corn, beans, and squash.

Other Indian tribes were the Fox, Sauk (SAWK),
Huron (HYOU•ron), and Ottawa (AWT•toh•wah).

The first explorers in Wisconsin came from France.
In 1634 Jean Nicolet (JAHN nick•oh•LAY), a
Frenchman, sailed south from Canada, which was then

controlled by France. Nicolet entered Lake Michigan. Finally, his large canoe approached land at Green Bay.

Now begins a funny story. There were no maps to show Nicolet where he was. He thought he might have sailed all the way to China! So he dressed in Chinese clothes to greet the people. Imagine his surprise when he was met by Winnebago Indians. The Indians were surprised, too. But they were friendly to Nicolet and his men.

Other French explorers arrived over the years. Then French fur traders came. These men gave kettles, blankets, knives, axes, and trinkets to the Indians. In return they got animal furs worth a lot of money. French priests came, also. They tried to make the Indians give up their own religion. They wanted them to become Christians.

The French people built tiny villages, called settlements. The chief French settlements were at Green Bay and Prairie du Chien (PRAYER • ee doo shee • YEN).

Many Indians felt that these outsiders were taking over their land. In 1712 the Fox Indians began fighting the French. Later England decided that it wanted to own Wisconsin. For many years *three* groups fought over the land—the Indians, the French, and the English.

England finally won this war in 1763. Now England ruled Wisconsin.

Fort Crawford Military Hospital, Prairie du Chien

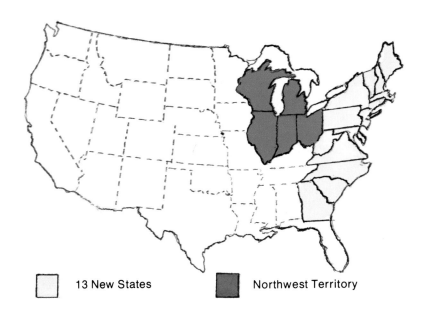

	13 New States		Northwest Territory

But this rule did not last for long. The people in
America didn't want to be ruled by England any longer.
They wanted to make a new country. They went to war
with England. This was called the Revolutionary War
(rev • oh • LOO • shun • airy WAWR). George Washington
led the American army to victory. A new, free country
was born—the United States of America.

Wisconsin became a part of the United States in 1783.
But it wasn't a state. It was a territory (TAIR • ih • torry).
It didn't have enough people to be a state.

In the 1820s, Americans began moving to Wisconsin. They had heard that there was a rich metal there. The metal was lead. Lead was needed to make bullets, water pipes, and paint.

The people who came to mine the lead were mostly men. Some miners did not bother to build houses. They dug tunnels into the hills and lived there, near the mines. "They are just like badgers!" people said. Badgers dig holes and live in them.

Some miners brought their families to Wisconsin. Families couldn't live in tunnels like badgers! Houses were built. Towns went up. Trails were made. Stagecoaches started coming to Wisconsin.

Some people became farmers. They grew wheat and corn. They raised milk cows.

All these newcomers pushed more Indians from their land. Some Indians fought. American soldiers were sent to Wisconsin. They built forts to protect the new towns.

In 1832 the Sauk Indians tried to regain some of their lands. That year, Chief Black Hawk led his people across Wisconsin. They were looking for a place to grow corn. American soldiers thought that Black Hawk was going on the warpath. They attacked the Indians.

The Indians fought back, but there were too many soldiers against them. Over a thousand of Black Hawk's people were killed. Chief Black Hawk and the few Indians who lived were locked up in a prison.

"I loved my towns, my cornfields, and the homes of my people," Chief Black Hawk said. "I fought for them."

After the Black Hawk War there were no more Indian wars in Wisconsin.

"There's great farmland in Wisconsin!" The word spread around the world. Settlers came from Germany and Sweden, Norway, and Finland. They built towns in Wisconsin much like the towns in their old countries.

By 1848 Wisconsin had 250,000 people—more than enough to become a state. On May 29th, 1848, Wisconsin became the 30th state. Madison was made the capital.

Iliam Tell Pageant, New Glarus

Do you remember those miners who lived in tunnels?
Because of them, Wisconsin became known as the
"Badger State." Wisconsin people became known as
"Badgers." The Badger State is 320 miles in its greatest
distance from north to south. It is 295 miles from east to
west. Lake Superior and a part of the state of Michigan
are to the north. On the east is Lake Michigan. To the
south is Illinois. Neighbor states on the west across the
Mississippi River are Minnesota and Iowa.

A big event happened very soon in the new state. The Republican Party was begun in 1854, in Ripon (RIP . awn), Wisconsin. It was started by people who wanted to end slavery in the United States.

Slavery was a big issue in the Civil War (SIV . ill wawr), 1861-1865. During this war the Northern states fought the Southern states. Many people in Wisconsin and the rest of the North were against slavery. Most in the South wanted to keep slavery.

There was no fighting inside Wisconsin. But 91,379 Wisconsin men fought for the North. The most famous Wisconsin soldier didn't wear a uniform. He was an eagle named "Old Abe."

Wisconsin soldiers bought the eagle from an Indian for five dollars. They named it "Old Abe" after President

Abraham Lincoln. Old Abe learned to carry a flag and to march. In battle the eagle would fly over the enemies' heads screaming at them. Finally, the South put up a reward for any soldier who could shoot Old Abe. Some feathers were shot out, but the eagle was too smart to be killed. Old Abe fought in 38 battles with the soldiers from Wisconsin.

By the time the North won the Civil War, Old Abe was a hero. People paid four hundred dollars just for one of Abe's feathers! The old eagle lived in the capitol building, at Madison. Many people came to see him, but Old Abe was happiest when his old soldier friends came to visit.

After the Civil War, lumber became very important. There were millions of trees in Wisconsin, most in the northern part of the state. There were sweet-smelling pines. There were tall, white birches.

Lumberjacks yelled *"Timber!"* as the trees fell. The lumberjacks worked during the fall and through the long winter. Winter was rough in the lumber camps. The temperature sometimes was 40 degrees below 0!

Above: Fall colors
Left: Nature trail in the Nicolet Forest

When all the trees in an area were cut down, the logs were put on sleds. Teams of oxen dragged the logs to the nearest river. When the weather got warmer, the lumberjacks started the "spring drive." They "drove" the logs down the river by pushing them along with poles.

Now and then a lumberjack cried "log jam!" That meant the logs were stuck. The strongest lumberjacks had to work hard to get them moving again.

Finally, the logs reached a sawmill town. At the sawmill, the logs were cut into boards. This wood could then be used to build houses and furniture.

The lumberjacks loved to tell tall tales. They made up stories about a giant lumberjack called Paul Bunyan.

You know that the lakes in Wisconsin were made by melting glaciers. "It was Paul Bunyan who *really* made those lakes," went one story. "First he climbed to the top of Rib Mountain. Then he jumped into the Wisconsin River. The big splash made all those lakes!"

They also said that Paul Bunyan had a giant blue ox named Babe, who could pull more logs than nine real oxen. "Babe needed a place to drink," went one story. "So Paul Bunyan dug Lake Superior for Babe."

All across the United States, lumberjacks made up stories about Paul Bunyan. But the Wisconsin lumberjacks made up some of the best.

Some people thought that Wisconsin would always have plenty of trees. But they were wrong.

The year 1871 was very dry. There were many forest fires that year. But the worst forest fire was around the town of Peshtigo (PESH • tih • go). The fire was so great that the sky turned red. Animals ran out of the forest with their fur on fire. Then the blaze reached the town. People jumped into the river to escape the flames. But 1200 people in the area were killed by the Great Peshtigo Fire. Fires like this killed millions and millions of trees.

Something else hurt lumbering. In some places the lumberjacks cut down *all* the trees. By 1900, many forests that had once been thick and green were bare.

The people of Wisconsin learned from these events. Forest rangers were trained to guard against fires. A law was made saying that when old trees were cut down, new ones had to be planted.

Today, Wisconsin's forests are mighty once more.

Like a young forest, Wisconsin grew rapidly in the 1900s. Farmers learned new ways to grow bigger and better crops. The cities grew, too. They became manufacturing centers—places where many things are made.

You have read about some of Wisconsin's history. Now you are ready for a trip through the state. You will see many places. You will learn about interesting people who lived in those places. And you will see what the people do today.

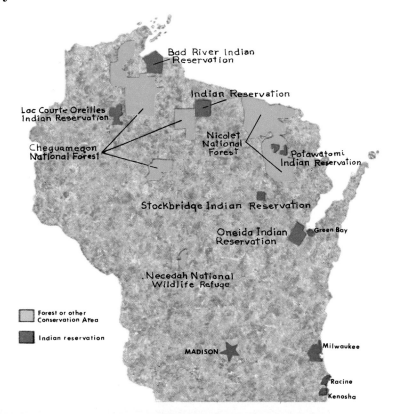

Bad River Indian Reservation

Indian Reservation

Lac Courte Oreilles Indian Reservation

Cheguamegon National Forest

Nicolet National Forest

Potawatomi Indian Reservation

Stockbridge Indian Reservation

Oneida Indian Reservation

Green Bay

Necedah National Wildlife Refuge

Forest or other Conservation Area

Indian reservation

MADISON

Milwaukee

Racine

Kenosha

A TRIP THROUGH WISCONSIN

"Look at all the cows!"

It is summer and the crops are green. Red barns dot the land. You see chickens and horses. And you see cows, cows, cows!

If a state could talk, Wisconsin might go "MOO!" Its two-and-a-half million milk cows make Wisconsin the leading state for milk. Can you read the words on Wisconsin license plates? They say "AMERICA'S DAIRYLAND."

ting—one step in cheese-making process

Milk ready to transport

In the 1870s, a Wisconsin man named William Hoard helped make Wisconsin a great dairy state. In those days, cows that gave milk were often killed for beef. "That's a waste," said William Hoard. He knew that a good milk cow can give over 1,000 gallons of milk a year. So why kill a good milk cow for beef? People listened to William Hoard. Now milk cows are separate from beef cows.

When your grandparents were your age, cows had to be milked by hand. Today, machines can do the job.

Many products are made from milk. Cheese is one of them. There are lots of cheese factories in Wisconsin, and they make every kind of cheese.

The biggest cheese *ever* was made in Wisconsin. It was a 34,591-pound cheddar cheese. It was taken in a huge truck from Wisconsin to New York, where it was shown at the 1964 World's Fair. Even Paul Bunyan couldn't have eaten this cheese. It was bigger than three elephants!

What do you put on your bread? What goes in coffee? Butter and cream are made from milk. Ice cream is made from milk, too. So the next time you eat an ice cream cone, remember the Wisconsin cows that made it possible.

Milk is not all that comes from Wisconsin. Sweet corn, green peas, cherries, apples, cabbages, and wheat are grown by Wisconsin farmers. And there's a good chance that the cranberries for your Thanksgiving dinner were grown in Wisconsin!

of Milwaukee with Performing Arts Center
eground

Cranberry Bog

Even though there are about 100,000 farms in
Wisconsin, most Badgers live in cities today. Do you see
those buildings looming in the distance? They belong to
Wisconsin's biggest city—Milwaukee (mill•WAW•kee).

Milwaukee is on the edge of Lake Michigan, near the
southeast corner of the state. Hundreds of years ago, the
Fox and Potawatomi Indians lived here. A fur trader
named Solomon Juneau (JU•noh) was the first outsider

to settle here. He came to Milwaukee in 1818 with his wife. The Indians liked to trade with Solomon Juneau, because he was a strong, fair man.

More traders came to Milwaukee. Soon settlers came, many from Germany and Poland. Milwaukee became a city in 1846. Solomon Juneau was the first mayor. The Juneau family was almost a city by itself. Solomon and his wife had *seventeen* children!

Milwaukee today is a great manufacturing city. Machines are made here. Food is packed here. Nearby Lake Michigan makes Milwaukee a great port city. Ships, loaded with goods, sail in and out of Milwaukee.

Milwaukee Zoo

The product Milwaukee is best known for is beer. You can visit a brewery and learn how beer is made. But you can't drink any. You're too young.

There are many fun things to do in Milwaukee. The Milwaukee County Zoo is one of the best in the world. The animals have lots of room. In the bird house bright-colored birds fly over your head. At the children's zoo you can feed the goats and sheep. This zoo has some of the best-looking animals you'll ever see.

Mitchell Park Conservatory

Have you ever wished you could see flowers in the middle of winter? You can in Milwaukee. In Mitchell Park there are three big glass bubbles. These are giant greenhouses. Inside one dome you can see the flowers and plants that grow in Africa and South America. The second dome is hot and dry like a desert. The third dome has flower shows throughout the year.

Milwaukee is a big sports city. In the winter you can see professional basketball. In the summer there is pro baseball. The greatest home run hitter of all time — Henry Aaron — played most of his career in Milwaukee.

Before you leave Milwaukee you must visit the Milwaukee Public Museum. Here you can learn about the Effigy Mound Builders and Wisconsin Indians. And be sure to walk through the "Streets of Old Milwaukee." It shows how Milwaukee looked in the early 1900s.

About 76 miles west of Milwaukee is the capital of Wisconsin. This is the city of Madison.

Madison is called the "City of Four Lakes." The state capitol stands on a hill between two of the lakes. Of all state capitols in America, this dome is the second tallest.

The front of Bascom Hall, University of Wisconsin

About a mile from the capitol is the great University of Wisconsin. Students here learn about many subjects. Some come to learn the newest ways of farming. That makes them better farmers when they return home.

Do you listen to the radio? The first radio station in America was started in Madison. Station WHA was begun at the University of Wisconsin in 1917. At first it just broadcast weather reports for area farmers.

No one knows who invented the very first automobile. One early auto was made in 1873 by Dr. J.W. Carhart. He called his funny-looking machine "The Spark." Wisconsin people claimed that the Spark was *the* first car.

Lawmakers in Madison saw that the car had a great future. In 1878 they decided to hold a 200-mile race from Green Bay to Madison. The winner would get $10,000.

Not only was this the *first* auto race, it was probably the funniest. Only two cars entered—one from Green Bay and the other from Oshkosh (AWSH•kawsh). People came from all over Wisconsin to cheer for their favorite. Both cars broke down a lot. Wheels fell off. They ran into ditches. After three days, the car from Oshkosh made it to Madison. It had only gone six miles an hour. You could walk that fast.

There is an old Wisconsin saying: "The world is your cow, but you'll have to do the milking." That means Wisconsin people believe in hard work. In cities across Wisconsin, people make things for all of America. Here are some of the products they make:

Appleton: paper and paper bags
Beloit: knives and saws
Eau Claire: concrete
Green Bay: cheese and paper
Janesville: pens and pencils
Kenosha: furniture, underwear, rope, cars
La Crosse: auto parts, rubber boots
Madison: hot dogs and other meat products
Manitowoc: furniture
Milwaukee: beer
Neenah: doors and snowmobiles
Oshkosh: matches and overalls
Racine: farm tools, waxes and cleaning products, books
Sheboygan: cheese and furniture
Superior: ships
Wausau: wooden toys, baby cribs, houses

The history of Wisconsin is seen in the names of its cities.

Milwaukee, Chippewa (CHIP•ih•waw) Falls, Manitowoc (MAN•ih•toe•wawck), and Oshkosh are just four of the cities with Indian names.

Eau Claire (oh•CLAIR), La Crosse (lah•CROSS), St. Croix (saynt•KROY) Falls, and Racine (ray•SEEN) remind you of the French period.

Green Bay is the oldest city in Wisconsin. In 1634 Jean Nicolet explored this lovely area. Shortly afterwards, French settlers made it their home. They called it Bay La Verte (bay la VAIRT). When the English came they called it Green Bay.

Ice boating on Green Bay

Today, Green Bay is the home of a famous football team—the Green Bay Packers. A lot of meat is packed in Green Bay. That's why the football team was named the "Packers."

The city of Green Bay is next to Lake Michigan. Products are shipped by boat in and out of the city.

Oshkosh is on the shores of Lake Winnebago, 85 miles northeast of Madison. In the early 1800s Oshkosh was a fur trading post. The town was named for a Menominee Indian chief.

Today, large and small wooden products from doors to matches are made in Oshkosh. Workmen all over America wear overalls that were made here.

Racine and Kenosha (keh • NO • sha) lie along Lake Michigan, close to the Illinois-Wisconsin border. Once, there was a lot of iron mining in northern Wisconsin. Much of this ore was shipped by boat to Racine and Kenosha. The ore was made into many metal products.

Today, metal products are still made in these cities. Over half a million cars a year are made in Kenosha. Many parts for cars are made in Racine.

Even with all its cities, Wisconsin is still half covered by forests. Many kinds of wildlife live in the forests. Can you read the signs that say DEER CROSSING?

Wisconsin has so many deer that drivers have to watch for them. Deer are shy, but maybe you'll see one peeking out at you from the woods. Bears, foxes, coyotes, badgers, raccoons, porcupines, and chipmunks also live in Wisconsin. There are even a few bobcats in the northern and western parts of the state.

Fishermen catch trout, pike, bass, musky, and perch in Wisconsin waters. Ducks and geese are fishermen, too. They live near Wisconsin lakes, where they can catch the fish they like. But Wisconsin gets so cold in the winter that the birds must fly south.

Left: Coffee brewing at big Muskie Jamboree in Boulder Junction

Below: Northern Wisconsin Lake

Stand Rock in the Dells

Wisconsin has many places of great natural beauty.

The Wisconsin Dells are about 45 miles north of Madison. The Wisconsin River made the Dells. The river cut through the soft sandstone rock. It took thousands of years.

Take a boat ride through the Dells. You'll pass some strange rock formations. They have strange names, too—like Devil's Elbow, Hawk's Beak, Witches' Gulch, and Fat Man's Misery.

Door County is a thumb-shaped piece of land that juts out into Lake Michigan. Many ships and sailors have been lost on the rocks off Door County. The place

Apostle Island

became known as "Death's Door." Today hundreds of people go to Door County for vacation. It has great fishing.

The Apostle (ah•POSS•ill) Islands in Lake Superior are a part of Wisconsin. To get to the islands you must go by boat from the town of Bayfield. People come from all over the United States to fish on the Apostle Islands.

Just two miles from Bayfield is a Chippewa Indian reservation. A reservation is an area set aside for the Indians. About 25,000 Indians still live in Wisconsin, mostly on reservations. Other Indian reservations in Wisconsin are at St. Croix (saynt•KROY) and Lac du Flambeau (LOCK doo flam•BOH), near Black River Falls, and in Menominee County.

You can visit the kindergarten at Watertown. It has been rebuilt to look just as it did in 1856.

Some states have a lot of gold or silver. Wisconsin's treasure has been its people.

Did you like kindergarten? In 1856 a lady named Margarethe Schurz moved from Germany to Watertown, Wisconsin. In Watertown she started a school for little children. She called it kindergarten (a German word meaning "children's garden"). This was the first kindergarten in America.

Have you ever used a typewriter? The first typewriter was invented in 1867 by Christopher Sholes, a Milwaukee newspaper editor. Two other men helped him. Sholes was not sure that the typewriter would be of much use. "I am afraid it will have its day and then be thrown aside," he said. What if he saw how many typewriters there are now!

Do you like the circus? The five Ringling brothers grew up in the town of Baraboo, Wisconsin. When they were boys, they had their own circus. Al did a juggling act with his mother's dishes. He broke just about every one. John danced. Their first circus animals were chickens, a goat, and a horse.

People liked the Ringling brothers' little circus. When the boys got older, they bought an elephant. They trained a bear to dance. In 1884 they started taking their circus around the country. It grew and grew until it became known as "The Greatest Show on Earth."

Circus World Museum, Baraboo

In Baraboo you can visit the Circus World Museum. Here you can see a lot of circus equipment.

Do you like magic? A magician grew up in Appleton, Wisconsin. He was Harry Houdini (hoo • DEE • nee). As a young man, Houdini worked in a circus. Then he became a magician. Houdini amazed people. He could free himself from handcuffs. He often had himself tied up in a box and thrown into the water. He was able to escape from the box. When Houdini came to perform in a town the first thing he did was have himself locked inside the jail. In a few minutes he would escape from that jail.

Even Harry Houdini's greatest magic tricks could never equal the enchantment of Wisconsin.

Blue lakes . . . mighty forests . . . the beautiful Wisconsin Dells.

The land of milk . . . cheese . . . ice cream.

Home to Indians . . . lumberjacks . . . farmers.

The great city of Milwaukee . . . Madison . . . Green Bay.

This is the Badger State—Wisconsin!

Winter Scene, Vilas County

Facts About WISCONSIN

Area—56,154 square miles (26th biggest state)

Highest Point—1,952 feet above sea level (Timms Hill)

Lowest Point—581 feet above sea level (along Lake Michigan Shore)

Hottest Recorded Temperature—114° (in 1936, at Wisconsin Dells)

Coldest Recorded Temperature—minus 54° (in 1922, at Danbury)

Statehood—30th state, May 29, 1848

Capital—Madison

Counties—72

U.S. Senators—2

U.S. Representatives—9

Electoral Votes—11

State Senators—33

State Representatives—99

State Song—"On Wisconsin!" by J. S. Hubbard, Charles Rosa, and William Purdy

State Motto—*Forward*

Nickname—Badger State

State Slogan—America's Dairyland

State Seal—Adopted in 1851

State Flag—Adopted in 1913

State Flower—Wood Violet

State Bird—Robin

State Tree—Sugar maple

State Animal—Badger

State Wildlife Animal—White-tailed deer

State Fish—Muskellunge

State Domestic Animal—Dairy cow

Principal Rivers—Mississippi and St. Croix (western boundary)

> Wisconsin
> Black
> Flambeau
> Milwaukee
> Peshtigo
> Fox
> Rock
> Chippewa
> Brule

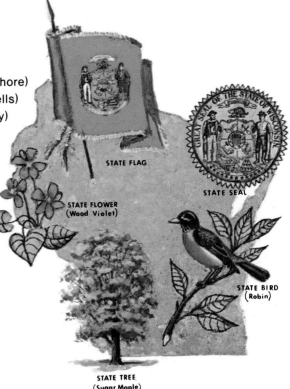

STATE FLAG

STATE SEAL

STATE FLOWER
(Wood Violet)

STATE BIRD
(Robin)

STATE TREE
(Sugar Maple)

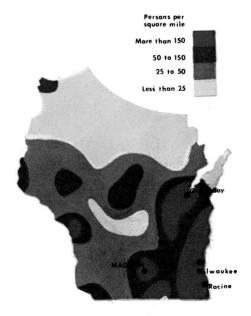

Persons per
square mile

More than 150

50 to 150

25 to 50

Less than 25

Green Bay

MADISON

Milwaukee

Racine

45

Highest Waterfall—Big Manitou Falls (165 feet)

Lakes—8,842 within state. The biggest is Lake Winnebago
(30 miles long, 10 miles wide)

Farm Products—Milk, milk products, corn, cranberries, green
peas, cherries, apples, cabbages, hay, eggs,
hogs, potatoes, wheat

Fishing—Muskellunge, northern pike, trout, perch, bass,
bluegills, sunfish, whitefish, smelt, carp

Mining—Granite, dolomite, iron ore, lead, zinc, basalt,
marble, sandstone, shale, quartzite, sand

Manufacturing Products—Paper, paper products, wood products,
electrical equipment, machinery, food products

Population—4,417,933 (1970 census) 16th most populous
4,669,000 (1975 estimate)

Population Density—83 people per square mile

Major Cities—Milwaukee (city only, 1970 census) 717,372
Madison 171,769
Racine 95,162
Green Bay 87,809
Kenosha 78,805

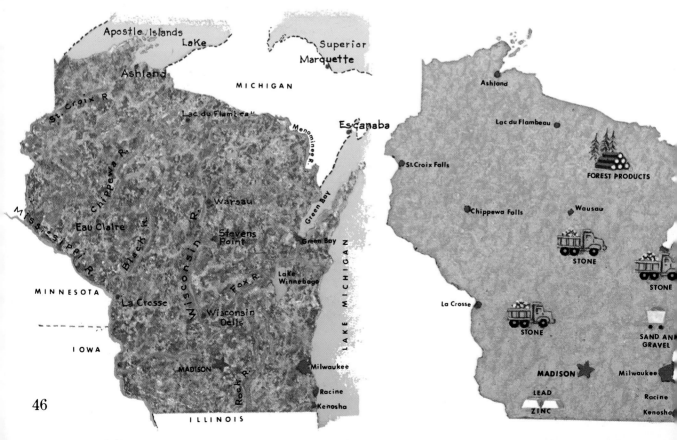

Wisconsin History

8000 B. C. —First evidence of people in Wisconsin

750 A. D. -1600—Indian group called "Mound Builders" in Wisconsin

1634—Jean Nicolet explores Wisconsin for France

1654-1656—French fur traders Groseilliers and Radisson in Wisconsin

1660—About this time Father Rene Menard came to Wisconsin; he was first missionary to Indians in Wisconsin

1671-1763—French rule in Wisconsin

1763-1783—English rule in Wisconsin

1818—Solomon Juneau goes to Milwaukee

1848—Wisconsin becomes the 30th state on May 29

1854—Republican Party is born at Ripon

1856—Margarethe Schurz founds first American kindergarten at Watertown

1861-1865—Civil War; 91,379 Wisconsin men fight for North

1867—Typewriter invented by Christopher Sholes of Milwaukee

1871—Great Peshtigo Fire kills about 1200

1872—William Hoard helps organize the Wisconsin Dairymen's Association

1873—J. W. Carhart builds automobile, "The Spark"

1878—First auto race, from Green Bay to Madison

1883—Malted milk invented, by William Horlick of Racine

1884—Ringling Brothers start taking their circus around the country

1890—Professor Stephen Babcock invents a method of measuring butterfat in milk

1915—Airplanes first used to patrol forests

1917—First radio station in U. S., at Madison

1917—Present State Capitol Building completed

1917—U. S. enters World War I; about 125,000 Wisconsin men and women in uniform

1919—Wisconsin is first state to approve law allowing women to vote

1924—Robert M. La Follette, Sr. runs for president as Progressive Party candidate, but loses

1932—Wisconsin becomes first state to pass an unemployment compensation law

1933—Wisconsin has first large soil and water conservation project in U. S. — in Vernon County

1939—Cave of the Mounds is discovered

1941—U. S. enters World War II; about 350,000 Wisconsin men and women in uniform

1948—Happy 100th birthday to Wisconsin!

1957—Milwaukee Braves win World Series of baseball

1961—Wisconsin becomes first state to pass seat belt law

1966—Wisconsin Bikeway completed, going from Kenosha to LaCrosse

1971—State lawmakers create the University of Wisconsin state university system

INDEX

About the Author:

Dennis Fradin attended Northwestern University on a creative writing scholarship and graduated in 1967. While still at Northwestern, he published his first stories in *Ingenue* magazine and also won a prize in *Seventeen's* short story competition. A prolific writer, Dennis Fradin has been regularly publishing stories in such diverse places as *The Saturday Evening Post, Scholastic, National Humane Review, Midwest,* and *The Teaching Paper.* He has also scripted several educational films. Since 1970 he has taught second grade reading in a Chicago school—a rewarding job, which, the author says, "provides a captive audience on whom I test my children's stories." Married and the father of two children, Dennis Fradin spends his free time with his family or playing a myriad of sports and games with his childhood chums.

About the Artist:

Robert Ulm, a Chicago resident, has been an advertising and editorial artist in both New York and Chicago. Mr. Ulm is a successful painter as well as an illustrator. In his spare time he enjoys fishing and playing tennis.